NOTICE: THIS MATERIAL MAY BE
PROTECTED BY COPYRIGHT LAW
(TITLE 17 U.S. CODE).

Riley Library
Northwest Nazarene

D0396622

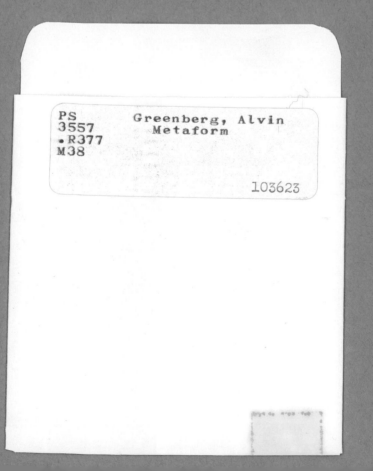

PS
3557
.R377
M38

Greenberg, Alvin
Metaform

103623

metaform

metaform

alvin greenberg

University of Massachusetts Press   Amherst 1975

103623

Copyright c 1975 by Alvin Greenberg
All rights reserved
Library of Congress Catalog Card Number 75-8448
ISBN 0-87023-188-X (cloth), 0-87023-189-8 (paper)
Printed in the United States of America
Library of Congress Cataloging in Publication Data

Greenberg, Alvin.
Metaform.
Poems.
I. Title.
PS3557.R377M38   811'.5'4   75-8448
ISBN 0-87023-188-X
ISBN 0-87023-189-8 pbk.

for Wendy Parrish

"the uninvited" is reprinted by permission from *American Poetry Review* 4, no. 1.

"last things," "grand tour," and "houdini at the gates of hell" are reprinted by permission from *American Review* 16.

"axiom" is reprinted by permission from *Cafe Solo* 12.

"command performance" is reprinted by permission from *Centennial Review* 16, no. 3, pp. 258-59.

"spring song" is reprinted by permission from *Dacotah Territory* no. 4 (Winter/Spring 1973).

"subdivision" is reprinted by permission from *Epoch* 22, no. 3.

"the natural history museum" is reprinted by permission from *Gegenschein Quarterly* 7/8 (1974). Copyright c 1974 by Phil Smith/*Gegenschein Quarterly*.

"metaform" and "closing in" are reprinted by permission from *Greenfield Review* 4, no. 1 (May 1975).

"problem solving" is reprinted by permission from *Iowa Review* 4, no. 2. Copyright c 1974 by Alvin Greenberg.

"visitation" is reprinted by permission from *Kansas Quarterly* 5, no. 3.

"the time machine" is reprinted by permission from *Little Magazine* 6, no. 2/3 (1972).

"at the little big horn" is reprinted by permission from *New American & Canadian Poetry* 22/23.

"star flight," "influences," "sungrazer," and "so?" from the poem "comet seeker " are reprinted by permission from the Spring 1975 issue of *New Letters* (41, no. 3).

"summertime" is reprinted by permission from *North Stone Review* 7 (Summer/Fall 1975).

"directions" is reprinted by permission from *Poetry Northwest* 13, no. 4. "dining out" is reprinted by permission from *Poetry Northwest* (Winter 1972-73). "to the man advertising in the 'personals' for a used parachute" is reprinted by permission from *Poetry Northwest* (Spring 1975).

"comet seeker" is reprinted by permission from *Poetry Now* 2, no. 3 (May 1975).

"slideshow" and "poem with obvious title" are reprinted by permission from *Seneca Review* 4. Copyright by Hobart & William Smith College Assn.

"house and garden" is reprinted by permission from *Snowy Egret* 37, no. 1 (1974).

The series "landscapes" is reprinted by permission from *Voyages to the Inland Sea* 4, University of Wisconsin-La Crosse Center for Contemporary Poetry, publisher; copyrighted and edited by John Judson.

"lawn party" is reprinted by permission from *Wind* 12 (1974).

contents

iv. landscapes

i among the dead and dying

last things

the salesman from the memorial society
offers me a better price now
than when i am dead.

do i want to bargain with him?
'sooner or later,' he says, 'you will.'

but i already belong to a society of death:

look at these hands: white and red:
what better credentials could you ask for?
onto my palms fall the world's
messages, delivered by the mailman

in the black truck. 'special delivery?'
i ask him. he says, 'no.'

houdini at the gates of hell

' i can dictate feelings to every inch of my body:
cure overnight the ulcer of my discontent,
tell those devilish hairs that crowd my anus
to leave off their tickling, leave off!

the key to this place i have secreted
somewhere about my person. i defy you
to find it. only the gland beneath my armpit
knows, my kidney, a certain muscle in my thigh:

i have burned this knowledge into them
with the fire of my passage, making myself
theirs. when they spit up the key, i

will come through that door. give me
three days: less would take a miracle.
when i return you shall not see me.'

dining out

across the street the lake begins to boil.
everyone suspects the chef,
recently arrived in the neighborhood,

who has received international acclaim
for his new entree: *l'homme flambé.*

while the lake simmers,
backyard gardens are raided at night.
rabbits no longer sit in the grass at dawn.
many things stir in the hissing waters.

when the dishes are washed we settle down,
in striped lawn chairs, before our houses,
in the bug-free evenings of october,

powerless and hungrier than before.
in the dense aroma the children rattle coins,

each one stamped with a hat and a rabbit.
'o we know where to spend them,' they say.

when it is dark, we go to bed,
fully clothed, napkins tucked in our collars,

ready at every moment for the bell
that calls us to this desperate cuisine.

autumnal

here a woman turns into a tree
and back again,

a tree a woman a tree a woman . . .
christ won't you hold still for a minute!

'take cold baths and long walks. alone.'

the forest is full of trees i know.

it rains and i receive
a cold shower of falling leaves.

lawn party

our host wears an old tuxedo, midnight blue,
his sneakers suck the flagstones dry,
'life,' he says, 'is all i have.'

on each of us he bestows, as we descend
from the veranda, a perfumed handkerchief:

lavender: the autumn sun draws forth its fumes.
the gate springs open when the hand draws near.
our pants legs whisper through the uncut grasses.
who brought us here we see no more. alone,

we wander among the bodies in the field,
among the snapped necks and torn shoulders,
the long stalks of legs chewed open to the bone.

'i wish,' you say, 'we had brought a mirror.'
the sun's claws catch in the evening sky.
i close my eyes.

when i open them, everything

is just the same. at the edge of the field,
beside the lake, the lions assemble. a figure
glides among them, black and white.

the lavender wind blows from us to them.

night visitor

'i do not promise to save you from sin.
i do not promise to save you
from the failure to sin.

i do not even promise to save you from yourself.

i say these things from the back of the lion.
his paws crunch in the gravel of your drive,
his head is already between the gates,
only the children sing his welcome:

do they see my hands buried in his mane?
i promised to return, didn't i?

i am back. when the children stop singing,
when the children are all in bed,
i will sing *my* song all night long.'

grand tour

this is the beginning: mark it well.
it has no end.
if it does, you won't know it.

here is the palacio municipal,
designed, it is said, by michaelangelo.
only the façade remains. or:
only the façade was ever completed.

here are various relatives, all mine.
here are various friends and enemies,
also mine.
they are having a party at which,
i suspect, none of us is welcome.
that mark on the door means 'no tourists.'

here are many empty rooms.

this is the place where we find
i-forget-who.
his eternal punishment is
i-forget-what.
you all know him.
please take care not to disturb him.

these creatures i have never seen before.

and here is the elephant graveyard
of the spirit. see:
nothing in it.

no, no pain. no pleasure either.
any further questions?

mid-winter

this is the most barren spot of all:
here, in the very center of things.

snow up to my crotch. no paved roads.

no tables, no rooms. no buildings. no
noise. no animals. only a few trees,

their bark worn—there: right at the snowline!—
by the dumb, continuous ritual of my passage.

subdivision

lot, *n.*: one's fate or 'a building site,'
as in 'the number of lots in this development

is limited, the size of individual lots
infinite. we build to suit. nothing cheap
or shoddy, you understand. all is tone:

entrance down a private drive, between
a pair of stone pillars, the stone head

of a lion on one, a giant bronze key on
the other.' the name of the place translates as
'he who marks the spot where the beast enters.'

the residents, whom you must remember not
to approach too closely, call it 'the candy veldt.'

on winter evenings from the lion gate
you can hear their voices on the clean, dry air

crying out the numbers of their addresses and
the tax assessor's crisp, pure, fractional figures.

the time machine

the magician is still lost in the depths.
much of the crowd that hung over the edge
has begun to wander away,

some even demand their money back:
what's so interesting about death?
there are other activities,
more musical, less lifelike,
than these bubbles rising slowly to the surface.

what can he be doing all this time?
will the moon, now rising, draw forth
the hasp from the rusty lock?
will he be disappointed that i, alone,
have awaited his return?

what will i say at dawn when,
not even rippling the still water,
he returns to perch in my left ventricle,
singing the song of the key?

the uninvited

in the darkened house we have fed
the midnight guest, who refuses the soufflé
but keeps on helping himself to the goulash.

pies, coffee, mints, all fail to attract him.
'my meals,' he tells us, 'never get that far.'

but now it is almost dawn. the neighbors,
passing on their way to work,
will see him seated in the kitchen window,

juggling the empty bottles of zinfandel.

we remind him of the empty guest room, above,
of the rooms all empty now except this one;
for the children have fallen asleep
in the corner, beside the refrigerator, amazed,

and we in our bathrobes sit and watch
the amber bottles that soar around his face.

through that boozy vertical halo the sun
comes up on the smile of a starving castaway:
truly seeing his companions for the first time.

spring song

it is the last of march,
perhaps the last of everything.

the snow deepens into spring.

i am an eagle eagle eagle
with a broken wing, denying
the blood spots on the snow:

not mine.

tomorrow i fly again.

'why is there something rather than nothing?'

the unmarked trucks of the exterminators
cruise the neighborhood.

they know it by sound and smell.
not even the silent, powerful toilets of the rich
escape their keen ears.
odors of death they nose out quickly.

shy fish among the darting delivery trucks,
their will be done. they don't ask questions:

they know what they do, they know how
to do it, they know why . . .

we see them from the still uncurtained windows:

they are the first to come and last to go.
new residents and old are equal in their eyes.
the dwelling place is all they care about.

at the little big horn

1. when my horse was shot from under me
   i would have gone down with it
   and then, at its final crumpling,
   rolled its shoulders across my own body
   and lain like that without moving
   for two days and two nights.

2. i would have fought on, to the very end.
   i would have shot everything, white and red,
   that passed between my sights.

3. i would have found my home in the tall grasses.

4. i could have brought the children.
   we could have watched it all from the high ridge.
   we could have stayed till it was all over,
   till even the last crows were gone,
   then we could have gone home ourselves and said,
   'we were *there*! we saw *every*thing!'

5. i could have thrown myself before the general's horse.
   i could have gone and talked to the others.
   i could have fled to washington, d.c.
   i could have done almost anything.
   i do not think i could have stopped this thing.

6. i am still there, my violet eyes
   ride the wavering tips of the milkweed plants.

command performance

this is the beast who says 'come with me'
in a voice that admits no refusal.

the invitation is embossed with the key
to my life, its motto 'open me.'

the key itself is shaped like a tree.
its roots probe every lock.

in the foliage perches a familiar beast
in the shape of a lion, his jaws open.

now he is silent. but his tongue is engraved
with a red invitation. when he leaps

we will be close enough to read it.

summertime

an early heatwave drives even the lion
back into the dark old bone of his lair.

if nothing is moving,
can there be any messages to deliver?

his tongue lolls in the dry sand.

the tourists, who come without weather
of any kind, do not interest him.

therefore we straggle along among them,
our cameras set to all the slowest speeds,
peering over their shoulders to read
guidebook comments on this 'superb' boneyard.

when they are gone, the sun falls.
the wind comes up across the dark lake.

presence to presence on the dry veldt,
we lie down together in the tall grasses.

directions

like a game-losing error, the magician
continues to haunt us. we find his key

in our mailbox, notched with promises.
we return at night to find messages
that he has phoned. should we be disturbed

that no one was home to take his calls?

we *are* disturbed. in the classified section
under 'personals' is a notice advising us
to contact him at once. at the intersection
is a sign reading 'MAGICIAN: 5 Km.'

the arrow points straight ahead. the light
changes. the cars behind us are honking.

metaform

the rock changes into a bird, the bird
into a pane of glass. things

seem to be improving: the landscape

behind the bird, on which the rock
formerly rested, now becomes the landscape
seen through a pane of glass.

the applause that follows is unwanted:

the suspicion that this is magic
is unfair. we ought not to be watched
so closely. we need the freedom

of the ordinary. only then
can the ordinary successfully happen.

closing in

the noose of the shoreline tightens
on the lake. pondweeds rise among the bones
of the fish, the beaver, the rabbits.

the great stew cools and thickens.
moss and sedges spread themselves upon it.

nothing that ever went down into it
rises again. no matter how long we wait.

the sunken chains are locked in peat.

now there is only one small circle
of open water left. with tamarack and poplar
we root in around it. across its dark surface,

where the sun falls along the marshy edge,
the lion stands, solemn and unblinking.

this amber pool feeds all our thirsts.

ii falling

humpty dumpty

how do these people who get thrown from moving vehicles survive?
who meet the earth at speeds at which the body explodes and yet
who do not explode—though perhaps the earth explodes before them?

what of the stewardess who falls seven miles into czechoslovakia
and walks—walks!—to work every day now—and her work is flying?
and what of my grandmother's sister who left a car at high speed
and sat on the road till they came back, the door still flapping?

and a woman i know who fell in a figure eight, impossible figure,
yes, two complete loops, one around her life and one around mine:
what did she find as she circled to let her rise and walk again,
stand up out of the earth, brush the dirt from her clothes and run
to catch up with where she'd have been if she had never fallen?

all my life such sudden models of behavior have fallen upon me,
from great heights, and got up and walked away and left me here,
perched motionless on the edge of myself, keeping so very still,
humming softly: i will not fall, i will not fall, i will . . . .

axiom: nothing is quite identical to anything else

when you first come upon the inland gulls
at lake superior, you wonder who is most lost:
you or them. all your life

you have taken the gull for a sign of the sea.
only now do you realize

that they fish the pond behind your house,
breed like ducks in the minnesota wetlands,
feed on insects in the plowed fields of nebraska,

that gliding across the pages of your history book
they sweep dry utah clean of grasshoppers,

that those curved wings slipping sideways
above you, white, motionless,
as if someone else put them there,

have absolutely nothing to tell you.

falling

still clinging tight, he said, we fell and fell

toward snow the softest landing. or water next.
save us from the earth: this cushion of flesh
is all there is to protect us, finally. all

except these little words we bind us up with,
which ask us, turning, tangled in our fall,
'do you think on death?' yes, we think on death

which quickly empties our pockets as we fall,
for these last principles of flight we know:
people fall. with them their worlds fall, too,

among keys, coins, cries of 'but we meant . . .'
yes, even in the fierce joy of their descent
the thing that holds them is, *it is*, a fall.
deep into the soft earth of themselves they fall.

sleeplearning

1.

in dreams i fall and do not wake.
morning finds me still falling.
the sun rises and sets on my fall.
i fall in a continuous circle
around the round world of my dreams.
i fall like a small planet, caught
in the gravitational field of dreams.
my orbit is as constant as a moon.
i chart myself and post the chart:
an aid to you midnight navigators.

2.

observe me through the atmosphere
of your own world, considering
the soft haze that surrounds me
as a clue to your own weather.
i'm as predictable as sin or money.
every move i make relates to you.
i'm either above you or below you.
all my sides i show you as i turn.
i'm only seen by reflected light but
the light i reflect isn't only mine.

3.

can you see anything in my falling?
will i finally hit like a meteorite,
burying the iron message of my fall
deep in the tundra of your own dreams?
can you match your speed, your orbit,
with mine? are you dreaming just now?
i don't even bother to dream anymore.
falling becomes my life. do you see?
and when you nod, 'yes,' do you feel
how the floor gives way beneath you?

the natural history museum

here you have one
of the final responses.
not just the words
about the response:
the response itself.

1.

this is the 20th century male, says the guide,
rapping his stick on the twin glass cases,
and this the female: *homo epistemologicus:*

he brought fire from the sun, and yet
warmed his hands in the pockets of her flesh.

2.

i myself am reconstituted from a single tooth.
it reveals how i have chewed my life.

to the man advertising in the 'personals' column for a used parachute

1.

boredom drives me to the want ads, ken,
the same way perhaps as it sends you
plunging through the clouds.

together we leap:
the weekend is spread out against the sky
in slender columns of grey type.

shall we trust ourselves to used desires?

2.

'free fall' is the only jumper's term i know.

it means, i think, spilling oneself recklessly
among shetland ponies, garage sales,
rusty trailers, out-of-work machinists.

the paper crumples as i dive toward it,
a flat landscape coming suddenly alive
in the deep erosions of nearness.

3.

down we come now, too fast, tangled
in worn strings, remnant fabric bargains.

i could have called you at 561-9607, ken,
and fallen free straight into your life,

arms spread wide, crying into the wind,
'ken, please don't buy a used . . .'

but i thought i'd write you a new poem instead.

visitation

in the spring our mother the wood duck
comes down the chimney—
that tall vertical bridge into our house—
to hide her eggs behind the piano.

we put her out at the front door,
an honored guest.
but adios, mother!
there are already too many eggs here,

too many bridges: they all lead in.
lower the gate! close the grate!

problem solving

the salad is on one side of the river,
still in the garden.
the salad bowl is on the other,
sitting beside the dressing on the table.
we are in midstream in a small boat.

consider:
we and the salad must not be in the boat together.
the dressing is non-transportable.
only a single crossing is possible.

moreover, the dog is in the water already,
swimming strongly, the tow rope in his teeth,
and the current carries us sideways,
ignoring the green signal of the lettuce,
the red of the tomatoes.   now:

pick up your oars! in the next chapter
we begin to deal in multiple unknowns.

yes

" 'That is the question . . . . How to
be! *Ach!* How to be.' "

Conrad, *Lord Jim*

1. how do we learn?

from the beginning: the spider in the crib,
the trail of crumbs on the forest path,

a cloud, another cloud, still another cloud,
the voice of the turtle suddenly translated.

nothing here that ever was before.

2. how do we travel?

above the clouds, the pilot older
than the entire history of manned flight,
his mind melting as we near the sun,

the crew silenced by the static of discovery,
last words in the true flight of the body:

this is your . . .
ground temperature now . . .
the center will (will not) hold.

3. how do we survive?

we are elephants in the country of habit.
we know where the water hole is.
where to sleep. where to die.

o the skin is thick with our behaviors.

4. how do we view the world?

how many *people* there are here!
everywhere: how many pieces!
the remarkable ways in which they are all broken!

the fine grit of humanity in the damp air
beside the pond, beneath the cloud,
gasping in the dark habits of the dream,

breathers dying of black heart disease.

5. again, how do we survive?

the corpse within us rises in the night
to direct the traffic of the living.

when it says *go*, the green light
spreads direction on our skins.

6. how do we talk?

thinking there's merit in everything we say.
even these words: remember them
whether or not we understand them.

someone may make good use of them.
anyone could have said them,
but we did.

7. how do we eat?

the wide comet of appetite approaching the sun,
first snow of winter salting the earth below:

for a moment, just now, we can define
what's yet to come, what's already behind.

then we begin the descent, the descent . . .

the center of everything loose in our midst.
inscription of teeth on flesh: *feel this.*

8. how do we spend our lives?

eating the earth. nursing our wounds.
forever cleaning up after ourselves.
capable of forgiving anything, perhaps.

purveyor of brooms and bandages,
the necessary god has many arms—and

one hand free. one hand wholly free.

9. and how do we go on from here?

may this poem come loose in your hand
like the gecko's tail when you grab it:

bloody, squirming, and alive.

iii   wind songs

wind songs

"Because of her I almost forgot butterflies
and completely overlooked the revolution."
        Nabokov, *The Gift*

1.

a wind came up where i once thought
there could be no wind,
curling over the high walls of the garden,

caressing the vegetables and lifting
the half ripened apples from the apple tree.

and because the door was open,

i left the house and walked in this wind
i left the house and walked in this wind
i left the house and walked in this wind

2.

did i turn my pockets inside out to the wind,
watching the lint fly?

i did.

did i turn myself about to the wind
and address the wind, saying, 'wind . . .'
and then falling silent?

i did.

did i grope about in this unusual weather,
thinking: who sees the wind sees everything?

o i did.

and did i power the loud lawnmower of despair
over the apples fallen in the tall grass?

yes, i did that too.

3.

love, as the blind see colors with their skin,
blindly i found my way by tongue and ear

across the cool body of the wind . . .

4.

is it, the wind asks, possible
to replace the wind?

no, it isn't possible to replace the wind.

there is no 'other wind'
there is only 'wind' and 'not wind'

and warm in the house where i live
not wind blows. this

wind irreplaceably hears.

5.

if one lives, in the midst of the wind . . .

if, in the midst of the wind,
one gathers others about oneself,
not to expose them to the wind,
not to protect them from the wind,
but to live with one, in the midst of the wind . . .

if, when the door is closed against the wind
and the windows locked
and the music turned up high
so that no sound enters from the outside,
one still knows one lives in the midst of the wind . . .

if, in the midst of the wind, one . . .

6.

why, you ask, is the great, now golden, maple
so still? the lake unbroken by a single ripple?

i confess: i have swallowed the wind.

in order to dine in a necessary calm,
without the napkins sailing from our laps,
the children whipped from their chairs, the salad
torn leaf by leaf from the battered salad bowl,

i have swallowed the wind.

in order to keep the necessary world
from blowing away, i have swallowed the wind.

i have swallowed the wind. in order to keep
the wind within me. i have. i have
swallowed the wind. in order to keep

in poems begin responsibilities

looking through old poems for the mole
on your right breast, i miss

an unexpected step—and the world trips,
spilling the green tray of summer.

spaceship july: everything floats,

gravity looking on like an uninvited guest,
clasping and unclasping its thin hands.

take a lesson in weightlessness:

turning the world upside down,
looking for your mark in the spaces

between the ordered stanzas of my life,
selves i never knew i had

drift around me in the shadow of the moon.

at night i lie awake beside them,
tucked in between my lines and yours,

working out the meaning of 'equilibrium.'

slideshow

these are the badlands, which i have carved
to resemble the deep erosions of travel.

this is a geyser: the moist question
it keeps asking is both yours and mine.

and here are the rockies, arched with loneliness,
great glacial lakes chilling their laps.

this is a rain forest, myself beneath the moss,
everything green and nothing moving.

this is the ocean but must be the wrong ocean:
those frozen waves don't move from you to me.

this is the desert. the desert speaks for itself.

and this is a metaphor and not
the desolate town in the middle of nowhere it seems;

above it stands the sun, that harsh projector,
waiting for the moon to move before it again,

cooling the long, western glare of summer.

lack of technique is everything

if 'when desire leaves the eye,
a man may see,' then i descend

blindly toward you here, feeling my way
down the hot ladder of july

in these slow, uneven lines,
no elegance to my passage, mirrors

laughing blankly as i clank by:
he doesn't know where he's going.

shhhh: never believe anything
with borders. that speaking image is

no longer me. see: i
already have one clumsy foot well beyond the frame

(and another set to follow).

and to what, except to you, do i move here?
the shadow of your world slides

at last across me, telling my skin
just where i am. soon i'll step down

on the soft ground of august, both feet
firmly embedded in the future.

> (quote from william gass,
> 'the stylization of desire')

house guests

they are led by children anxious to get their hands
on the coloring book of my life.

in minutes my outline is all filled in:
everything is blue and yellow and red
and there are no empty spaces anywhere.

i am become the man of primary colors,
and i speak with the wisdom of crayons, saying:

this, which the adults lift to their eyes and admire
this, which frees us now to turn the page
this, which is neither art nor life

burns, when the children sleep and the parents
move through the evening retrieving broken crayons,
with a quiet flame. in it

there are hidden corners which only the moon,
lifting the pages when the month is done,
can color in with shades of gold and brown.

and even the outline—the outline most of all!
expect nothing of the outline:

it flows like ink when the book is closed.

lines written on a paper plate

(at battle creek park)

when the sun begins to bend toward friday evening
and the thunderclouds spread their commentary
like mustard on the western horizon,

i find myself again where i am not.

down on the sand floor of this small canyon
the demon of the crowded picnic table,
struggling to fill my absence
with thin slices of conversation,

threatens to ambush me here in fifteen years,
unchanged—here
where forty indians died, one for each of my years.

fifteen years! my glass is full but my plate
is empty. the breakable words you see here
are the home-made cookies of loneliness:

small and dry, i share myself
with the absent indians. we crunch. you hear us.

the rain begins.

the ghost in the gallery

silent, without you, i walk the empty galleries,
venus and the virgin signalling me from the walls:

the one turning distastefully from an impossible child
and the other lifting one hand, palm out,
against the monstrous cupid at her feet.

if, as the catalogue claims, they know, these two,
precisely the freedom of the empty gallery

if, in my vague presence, they can arise
from the blurred, uncertain line,
from clumsy frames and impoverished neighbors

turning and turning in the darkened gallery

i think i'd better have you here beside me:

you to sit on the stone bench writing, in whispers,
the iconography of the unobserved

you, impatient among french masters at their worst,
dictating possibilities to my skin

you because, when you speak for me,
i say the most remarkable things.

poem with obvious title

i myself am the first bridge:
bridge of the body, crossing
the body, into the body.

i raise myself to let the world
pass through. i span
everything, link all that happens.

when there are tolls to pay, i
pay them.

but the earth is a bridge too,
leaping the gap between our hands,

and the flower is a bridge
into the dark veins of the plant.

even the potato is a bridge,
spinning its way onto my plate:
to cross it is to return to the earth.

i am not entirely reckless of bridges,
but some, like you, i could cross
and recross all day long,

never knowing which of my selves
you lead me to.

only at night, camping in the fog
on the far shore, do i think
of the dark waters running beneath you.

house and garden

see that stranger out there
in the garden, cultivating
his spring madness,

thinking he can keep it
blooming all year round:

maybe he's right.

let's lie down in the grass
and watch him, eating every
four-leaf clover we can find,

lucky in our bodies, which are
with us wherever we go.

walking the wide field
of the palm of your hand,
we count the digits one by one:
earth, grass, fern, clover . . .

clover, like the hand itself,
something to bend down to:

its taste precedes me
across the dark dakotas, high
in the rockies becomes a dream.

'a dream of what?' you ask.

simply a dream of clover:
a dream of the taste of clover
in the wild fields of your hands
waiting for me wherever i go.

comet seeker

1. comet seeker

rising at five a.m. to page through blank tree limbs
in search of a certain star not a star
a moving force that reaches from here to here in the night

yes: standing in the back yard in thin pyjamas in november
reading the book of winter already open, themes announced
rabbits bursting away from this spot in all directions

climbing the hill to unreel the scroll of the horizon
under the iron message of stars straight above
its full circle blurred in the glow of nearness

saying where are you where are you i know you're there

2. star flight

here's the round absence of everything. vortex
of possibility: dark hole of the future
into which my everyday absence is, every day, sucked

this simple. simple pull of space. named, empty space
scratch paper of my old skins whipped away
by its quick suction faster than i can shuck them

here everything happens faster, faster: absence
a cloud blotting star after star after star . . .
infinite acceleration at this triple crossroads

where i am and am not and you are

3. influences

astral phenomena, friend, auroras of unmeaning
tomorrow's stars visible in daylight
tonight's moon leaning right against the house

i found it there or did i put it there myself
listen: i found it there i think
radiant nocturne. let's visit the backyard

everything right where i put it. right
confession and discovery: cosmic householder
i am hostage to many gravities

who staggers heavily between this pull and that

4. passionate scenario

reported: one cannot breathe in outer space
the air's polluted. no, schmuck, there isn't any air
talk to me anyway. i await your breathless words

breathlessly. this, naturally, a monologue
airless as poe's best tomb. but space, what space!
a view terrific as the conversation. yes and

gasp. guess who lives here. gasp. alone
on location. no stand-in. orbits, wheezing, himself
signals direction. quiet. places. action. gasp

ms. found in a bottle. if human, break glass

5. approaches

through space like an arrow the arrow flies
daily everyone rising a half hour nearer to it
late sleepers. exhausted! forever catching up

is me, dear merciless comet. just waking, as usual
thinking children, food, clothing, words
daytime, see: fully illuminated from within

i brush my teeth before i raise the blinds. i do
o christ the house's in orbit. tracking a shower of gold
after it! after it! barks my dog zeno

closer each time by half'll never never be enough

6. anti-matter

so where did this sudden universe come from
erupted. merely to step outside for a moment and then
from the wrong end of someone's telescope

the sheerest invention. and full of populations
in my own livingroom everything
everything everything everything everything, yes?

i give you, here, the law of expanded matter:
today the rabbit follows me inside. tomorrow . . .
no magic, no lenses. just this, approaching farce

i am appeared, love, among you. a sudden universe

7. *two into one won't go*

today we number both universes and their possibilities
the board. the chalk. benign complexity of x and y
real heavenly bodies in this sketchy algebra

crying the fate of their own predicted orbits
begging return to the dark backyard. backyard before that
where each is center to a simpler mathematics: mine

here: standing in the backyard in thin pyjamas in november
moving outward among the rabbits. dropped chalk. stars
reading the wide fiery trail each leaves behind

stepping away from the board. smearing the unfinished . . .

8. *as clearly seen as possible*

in what great pudding does this all take place
whose sentences do not diagram nor metaphors equate
where early risers aren't up early enough

which meddles with their orbits. o it's not safe
what wanders about, untracked, in all this space
menaces the regulars. befuddles all. or nice

how this mix of language is stirred and stirred
thickening by halves. halves of halves. not hard
finally more a twilight or sunrise softly congealed

beneath whose light skin of words a shape's revealed

9. *sungrazer*

and from what distances, to this, are we come
wringing our hands in the primal stuff of the universe
incredible density. such a spray of phenomena we are become

by whose wide surprising trail the world itself interprets
o tell me again the story of our elliptical beginnings
orbits crossed. the heavy gravity that dictates our turns

everywhere in this semi-legible scrawl, with you, i am
reading the close, deliberate inscription of the sun
far side emergence. evening. are we seen? is it done?

all orbits we cross again: this one and this one . . .

10. *predictability*

one's shuffled from east to west, back yard to front
old known event. by some order possible to define?
reported, magnified, examined and not to be let go of

whispers of the future, too. orbit of aches and sighs
yes, but who's got an eye on the unfinished, correct design
and whose is that wasted over-the-shoulder glance

backwards being the answer no question calls for
all's extrapolation: so where's that damned dotted line
seeks me, friend, me: a regular schedule on which

the world recurs. once every lifetime. yours. mine.

11. so?

so: standing in the front yard in january in the evening
cold: i see nothing. nothing revealed as promised here
but because your light will come and come again

around me, however gross and remarkable the times, i exist
like a monument to an historical event which hasn't yet
occurred. but will. o will. i tell you, friend . . .

does rumor have it one takes his cosmos too too seriously?
well, without i do so, it's got no meaning, eh?
or means itself: the same. but's reflective, now, and bright

and *that* significance precedes me—us—through the night

iv landscapes

miscellaneous landscape

the cyclist who lifts the turtle from the road,
carrying home the orange and black shell
that the sunday traffic would soon have crushed,

the lake from which that turtle crept ashore,
haze of the city from which the cars have come
and implications of prairie in the uncut grass:

the poem is simply what is seen, lending
some coherence to all that moves through it,

an order for the fragments of the visible.

like the paired sight of binoculars, its lines
converge by design on the most distant object:

see those hills? close up, nothing's left of them
but figures, bushes, weed clumps: the landscape,

face to face, no longer a landscape at all.
something happens. the poem's what's strictly seen.
don't mistake coherence for life. that turtle,

rescued from onrushing cars in the first stanza,
is killed, before the last, perhaps by a dog,
in the night, between the lines. no one saw it.

can you, then, given the poem as it is, hold
these powerful binoculars steady in your hands?
will you rest them on my shoulder, leaning softly

against my back? can you, leaning into me, hold
these fragmented landscapes steady in your mind?

the poem is simply who is seen: you, leaning
your whole body into this dense chaos of mine.

landscape: the prairie

it's the great american failure,
like esperanto: no one speaks it anymore.

it was the language of dreams,
forgotten as soon as the dreamer awoke,
its slow rhythms chopped up into useful terms:

eat, buy, plant, build, kill, sell, go . . . .

like grass we didn't plant it thrusts up now
through cracks in the new sidewalk.

this always happens, so we can ignore its meaning,
turning it into an academic exercise:

we teach it to schoolchildren like latin,
and all that sticks is the flat phrase meaning

dead, dead, dead, dead, dead, dead . . . .

we teach them how to stand outside in the evening,
watering the sidewalk, not the grass,

and when they grow up and it becomes midnight
and when they pace the dark house listening
to the soft accents of their children breathing

and hear the muffled breath of the prairie
picking like dreams at all their locks,

they think: we know your meaning, we do.
what we don't know is . . . what you refer to.

landscape: the lake

there are three totally different poems here.

the first in which the water rises and falls,
with the season, a small lake, like myself,
with no outlet, a bathtub without a drain:

whatever happens fills it to the brim.

in mid-summer you can just see, above it,
the fine haze of evaporation: experience
surfacing vaguely over it like a poem.

a second which vibrates with the flight of ducks,
whose surface records what ducks have done to it:

the scars of the long wakes of ducks landing,
the snags of ripples closing over ducks diving,
froth torn up by the wingbeat of ducks ascending.

this is a badly damaged lake. with icy lines
it tries to close over itself, like a poem.

and a third in which the ice goes slowly out
and the water warms to me. the ice goes out.

it abandons the shore. wind directs its retreat.
ice darkens to the water it becomes. the lake

is a lake again, waters risen with the season.
we are full, full, full, full, full . . .

no outlet? we'll simply overflow, like a poem.

landscape with nesting figure

see that man in the corner, behind the sofa,
gathering twigs and bits of string?

like a startled pheasant his delusion
whirrs up among canapes and cocktail glasses,

his presumption of comfort a target for laughter
among these, his own sophisticated guests.

he himself remains below—building, building—
and as dull at recognizing natural enemies

as a creature prepared to become extinct.
he's yesterday's bird—still presentable

but shabbier than anyone else at the party.
wearing the brown suit of his determination

he wedges into the chinks of the final stanza,
as if it were a real world with a real future,

the toothpicks, olive pits, and peanut shells
you've been so busy hurling at him here.

darkening landscape

the air is so heavy with rain
even taste and odor grow soggy.
when i read from this damp card

the recipe for hungarian goulash,
no ingredients announce themselves.
weather dominates everything.

there's a cloud in the west
black as a full eclipse of you
that says: 'night, go hungry,

power lines all fall down now,
what do you need, what need?'
we pass, in silence, pots, salt,

fumbling among knives and meat
with each other's fingers.
what we do says what we need.

we have to eat and eat and eat:
our bodies thunder appetite
no matter what the weather says.

perhaps it is night already
and we are cooking in the dark,
practicing for blindness.

foreign landscape

we who move out of our dreams across the dark
borders of night, we who smuggle our dreams
in the hollow chambers of our hearts, we

whose every gesture is stuffed with contraband,

whose eyes violate the security of the awakened
and threaten to devalue brick and stone . . .

does the citizen feel cheated who buys from us,
overpaying for what might have been his own?

he hears us ticking loudly in the night, thinks:
we walk the streets like ordinary citizens.

well, let no one be fooled if we are seen

strolling hand in hand at the hour of promenade
or sharing, in the open restaurant on the square,
tastes of each other's food. each other.

and let no one be fooled by the way we speak
the language, or by our casual manner
with the currency and politics of daily life.

we are always in a foreign country. this landscape
no one knows. evenings, in the park we sit,

delicate containers of dreams lethal as bombs.
when it grows dark we close our eyes: go home.

landscape: family life

the world is studded with signposts: this

woman, for example, alight with direction,
one corner of her mouth turned up, the other
down, solidly imbedded between these lines.

why, the traveler who pauses here is himself
a sign, as his children are signs, who mingle
in the crowd at this confusing crossroad.

and the open window in the house by the road
is a sign. and the lake is a sign. and you
are a sign. and you and you. and the container

of all these signs itself a sign which says:

we must all identify each other correctly,
devouring the contradictions of stop and go,
planting ourselves along the dangerous curves.

only then can we decipher our own directions,
reading 'everything leads to everything else.'

landscape: the mind

everything here is created purely from memory:

the grass an improbable green and mountains
in the even, purple rows of a child's drawing.

nothing moves. the sky is carefully arranged,
the tree dead center. august stills the birds.

it is all done by mirrors, in which everything
belongs to something else: except that arm,

lying still there, the long fingers curved
across the pale breast, which i assign to you.

nothing moves here. neither the iron furniture
of memory—lawn chairs by a grey-green river—

nor the rain forgotten in the distant clouds.
the sky colorless, the tree still, dim thunder

of possibility as faint, behind the mountains,
as the mark of your fingernail on your breast

when i raise your hand in mine. nothing moves,
yet the mark fades. your skin turns as smooth

as the memory of the future, creating itself
like clouds, unseen, like the mirrors in which

i turn this poem, once pure and still as memory,
into you, only you moving across this landscape

i inhabit like a man holding his breath forever.

ultimate landscape

this is the landscape after making love.
here the earth throbs like the pulse in your neck,
a miniature in which everything resides.

and what's outside it? anyone there who speaks
the language of lakes and hills, or turns
the great machinery of memory toward the future,

detecting its quick, erotic pulse?

here, in miniature, in the corner, we reside.
no tools but ourselves do we have
for chipping away at the firm container of the frame:

the landscape's simply who is seen.

well, like that quick, erotic pulse in your neck,
the earth throbs beneath us as we work.
everything joins us here at the edge.

and when the borders have been crossed at last,
when the loud ticking of dreams disturbs the future,
when speech and the unspeakable reside together

and memory begins to create itself anew: everything
here will spread quickly outward, this landscape
enlarge upon the throbbing silences,

and there will be no container for this thing.